Veteran and Vintage Cars in Color

# Veteran and Vintage Cars in Color

Introduction and notes by Michael Sedgwick

A STUDIO BOOK

THE VIKING PRESS · NEW YORK

Published in 1971 by The Viking Press, Inc.
625 Madison Avenue, New York, N.Y. 10022

SBN 670-74560-x

Library of Congress catalog card number: 77-101790

Printed and bound in Denmark by F. E. Bording Ltd, Copenhagen

# Contents

# Acknowledgment

The Author and Publishers wish to thank Baron Raben-Levetzau for permission to reproduce the illustrations appearing in this book.

All the cars which feature in this volume can be seen at the Raben Car Collection in Aalholm Castle, Denmark, which contains more than 300 historic vehicles, and is open to the public annually from Easter until the Fall.
Half of the Photographs were taken by the Baron Raben-Levetzau.
The Publishers also wish to express their thanks to Mr J. Bache for permitting the reproduction of his photographs which appear on pages 17, 19, 21, 23, 25, 31, 33, 35, 37, 39, 41, 43, 45, 47, 49, 51, 53, 59, 63, 65, 67, 69, 79, 81, 83, 91, 93, 103, 117, 121, 137 and 143, and to The Castrol Oil Company in Copenhagen for providing the remaining illustrations, also to Mr Emil B. Arendt of Copenhagen for his help and cooperation in the publication of this book.

# Introduction

Why are we mesmerised by aged motor cars, be they spidery Benz 'Velos' or 'Phantom III' Rolls-Royces? Why do we restore them, polish them, rally them, gape at them in museums, read learned articles on their origins, and pay too much for them at specialist auctions?

Already our sport has its publicists, and they will argue that this vogue is a reaction from the uniform respectability of the modern automobile. One climbs in, turns the key, engages first gear (or, more probably, a position on the selector labelled 'drive'), and one is off, without benefit of starting-handles, starter buttons, sight-feed oilers, ignition controls, or even choke knobs. Diversity of layout is confined to things that *should* be uniform, such as horn and wiper switches, which can be anywhere according to the whim of ergonome or computer. But otherwise a car's behaviour is governed far more by the temper of those who put it together than by some lapse in the design department—we all know the 'Friday afternoon' model with its defective fuel gauge, ante-natal rust in the guttering, and orange-peel cellulose. Inbuilt, self-conscious safety also carries a ring of the punitive: one feels that the manufacturer is wagging his finger at the customer, and telling him that he is wayward, wilful, headstrong, and stubborn. It is perhaps wrong to jest over this, but not all such preventative devices are life-savers—in 1934 the pioneers of the unforgivable umbrella-handle handbrake hung a 'safe' label on this doleful creation.

In any case, does motivation matter, except to sociologists? We drive these cars because we like them, and not for form's sake, otherwise those fakes and replicas on modern chassis, from lawn-mower-engined

Curved Dash Oldsmobiles to pseudo '1750' Alfas by Zagato, would have sold much better than they did. We are also fast growing up to a point at which we no longer look to any particular club or nation as the *arbiter elegantium*, and this is reflected in the literature of motoring. Time was when certain cars were 'in', and anthologised beyond the best of Wordsworth or Shakespeare's sonnets. Others—which meant anything American in Britain, most things British in America, and any car built by a non-U maker after 31 December 1930—were just as firmly 'out'. Much of this chauvinism was commonsense run riot—for pure fun give us a $4\frac{1}{2}$-litre Bentley rather than 141 c.c. less of swept volume and two more cylinders from Derby—but it failed to take into consideration the increasing rarity and consequent inflationary value of the desirable, and also the rise of a new generation and a different outlook. Also, let us face it, there is a difference between a car that is a commercial proposition as transport, and one which was apparently brought into being for the delectation of latter-day collectors. Present-day scarcity may result from an owner-loyalty that caused a breed to be kept for ever or driven into the ground: it may equally be the consequence of fragile bottom-ends, servicing headaches beyond the endurance of the every-day motorist, or merely premature abandonment because the manu-facturer found it didn't pay.

National chauvinism is a perilous thing, and only in the selective 1960s has the motorist once again demanded (and got) a choice of breeds from every country. At the present time a Briton can take his pick from the wares of Australia, Canada, Czechoslovakia, France, Germany, Italy, Japan, the Netherlands, Scandinavia, Switzerland, the United States and the U.S.S.R. Hence his knowledge, both theoretical and practical, tends to be greater, and in 30 years' time the motoring historian (who is supposed to know about every car, but seldom does) will be superfluous. When one encounters Skodas in small British towns, Volvos in American ones, Hillmans on the cab-ranks of Milan, and Volkswagen everywhere, it is clear that prejudice is being cast overboard.

Let us, however, cast our minds back to, say, the 1930s, and consider the score. Relatively few foreign makes were on general sale in Britain or America, and not many manufacturers who exported to either country offered more than a cross-section of their ranges. Nor did they always bear the same *cognomina* as at home. Horse-power calculations varied from country to country, and what the French called a 5CV Citroën was known outside France as a '7·5 h.p.' Worse confusion ensued: the Gallic *sept chevaux* was an English Twelve, and the Quai de Javel's *quinze* was a larger, longer, heavier, and more formidable confection than a Fifteen as assembled on Slough Trading Estate. Not a few Englishmen bought de Sotos and Plymouths under the impression that they were buying Chryslers, a Talbot was a Darracq, and in the Golden Age an Italian Florentia, a Belgian R.S.B. or La Locomotrice, and a Swiss Martini were all Rochet-Schneiders of Lyonnaise parentage under the skin. Whereas the internationalism of today's collectors, who shop all over the world, has ensured that any big Veteran or Vintage Rally will produce a satisfying variety of vehicles, in the past even an *aficionado* with a well-lined pocket could miss out on some gems. By the middle 1930s the Alvis had reached its zenith, yet it was unknown to Americans, and the great days of the Pierce-Arrow and Locomobile were passed over in Europe. As it was, the former carried vague associations with the Presidential motorcades of Harding and Coolidge, while the latter was recalled, reluctantly, as a primordial steam runabout with an apocryphal water consumption. The exigencies of German and Italian economics excluded anything outside the realms of cheap licence-production or the entry-lists of the *grandes épreuves*. Russians and Japanese seldom encountered a private car, Czechoslovakia possessed a compact, self-contained and well-protected industry, and only in countries combining a sound currency and negligible domestic production—Australia in the 1920s, Belgium, Sweden, or Switzerland—was the enthusiast's scope genuinely international.

The history of the motor-car has been written to death, yet once one has strayed beyond the well-trodden path of Cugnot, the Bollées, Daimler, Benz, Levassor, and Lanchester, there remains the appalling question: 'What should one include, and what should one omit?' Historic significance sometimes clashes with the truly representative. The Panhard was the archetype of 60 years of conventional automobile practice, but a 1903 model, for instance, does not represent the state of the art in Europe in what was the heyday of the Mercédès. Viewed in terms of U.S.A. design, it is even less representative, since American industry had yet to emerge from the chrysalid stage, as symbolised by Oldsmobile, Rambler, Northern, and their countless fellows. Nearer the present, Ford's Model-T outnumbered everything else in 1912, but as regards specifications it was hardly the 'average car': in its peak production years (the early 1920s) it was, in fact, so much the odd man out that some States offered two types of driving-licence—for planetary and orthodox transmissions respectively.

How, then, does one anthologise the cars of the past? One must resist a temptation to serve up the enthusiast's favourite menu, leavened with a few Old Faithfuls such as the Austin Twelve and the Bullnose Morris—scampi seven days a week can become tedious. One must resist even more firmly the urge to pander to purely national prejudices.

This book does not set out to be a potted history of the motor-car. Nor is it intended as a study of the automobile's evolution from 1902 to 1939, though it embraces vehicles spanning this era. The idea has been to present a cross-section of models, orthodox and heterodox, fast and slow, esoteric and commonplace, of the sort that might have been encountered in an 'ideal' market—i.e. one where the buyer could draw on factories from all over the world. I have been fortunate in having the co-operation of Baron Raben-Levetzau, proprietor of the Raben Car Collection at Aalholm Castle, Denmark, which is a collection with an international flavour.

Not that the Old Masters have been ignored, for the one-lungers of Cadillac and de Dion-Bouton, the Model-T Ford, the 'Silver Ghost' Rolls-Royce, Hispano-Suiza, Bugatti, and Packard find their places within these covers. But there are other less familiar faces to vary the fare. If one's tastes run to the elephantine, what price the 40CV Renault and the Locomobile, both with more than eight litres? The 1935 Cadillac, if their inferior in sheer swept volume, ran to 16 cylinders, and peculiarities in the transmission department embrace Holsman's Heath Robinsonian cables and pulleys, the friction-and-chain drive of the 1915 Metz, Chenard-Walcker's double-reduction axle, and the Stanley's simple power unit geared directly to the back end—'automatic' without the prolixities of a fluid coupling. As early as 1905 Lagondas had brakes of a sort on all wheels, even if there were only three of them, and the passenger-seat represented the nadir of peril and discomfort; yet in 1928 some Franklins presented the extraordinary combination of a wooden chassis and hydraulic braking!

*Marque*-names may be familiar, but the product can puzzle. The truckish 1909 Delahaye is a far cry from the handsome Type-135 sports car of the 1930s and 1940s, while it is hard to believe that only 12 years separate the last of Maxwell's austere flat-twins from their descendants, the advanced Chrysler '70s' of 1924. An even less credible contrast is furnished by the 1914 A.C. 'Sociable'—can this have any connection with the *gran turismi* which now emanate from Thames Ditton? In 1928 Opel were on their way up, and their wares were dull and innocent of the individual touch: de Dion, by contrast, had almost reached rock-bottom, a state of affairs reflected only too clearly by their 1925 offering. There is nothing in the outward aspect of the 15CV Lorraine-Dietrich tourer to suggest that an almost identical model beat the Bentleys at Le Mans on two occasions. The 1930 Renault suffers by contrast with its baroque forebears, and a post-war generation extending from the 4CV to the '16'. Anthologists have side-stepped the magnificent '853' Horch in favour of the 540K Mercedes-Benz—maybe because apparently no two cars from Zwickau bear the same type designation! And for sheer obscurity, it is hard to beat the Delaugère from Orléans, which remained but a name outside its native *département*, though it was said that you could still buy one in 1926. One wonders if anyone did, and what it was like. . . . .

Every model, however, has its adherents, even the mass-produced and commonplace. The colleague who said: 'I like her: I know just what she'll do, and what I can do with her', was speaking of a 1967 family saloon with 37,000 miles on the clock and only a Bosch spotlamp to distinguish it from myriads built to the same specification and colour-scheme. One cannot summon up affection for a vehicle just because it has a wheel at each corner and a eulogistic label attached by latter-day historians and Vintage fanatics. Some there are which one would drive only under protest—but no true lover of the motor-car would deny the right of others to cherish, preserve, and even enthuse in office or bar over his (or her) fancy.

The Plates

## HOLSMAN, 1902

The ensemble suggests the world of *Oklahoma*, though in fact the Holsman hailed from Chicago. It anticipated the high-wheeler craze of 1908–9, and was designed to go places where the fragile Oldsmobiles and Ramblers could not venture, hence the 48-inch driving wheels and their steel tyres. Running gear was pure buggy, the engine a simple air-cooled flat-twin, and the transmission a crude cable-and-pulley arrangement. The brakes also followed horse-carriage practice and even at 15 m.p.h. the ride was uncomfortable. Nevertheless, at $600 the Holsman filled a gap in the market, and sold at the rate of 900-odd a year: it also acquired a following in other countries afflicted with execrable roads, and examples survive in Australia and New Zealand.

## RAMBLER, 1902

Early American light cars were buggy-styled town runabouts: their flimsy construction was feasible if only because the country roads were quite beyond such vehicles. Oldsmobile was the great name, but in Wisconsin the Thomas B. Jeffery Co. were building up a steady reputation with their Rambler, which sold 1,500 in 1902, as against 2,100 of Ransom Eli Olds's masterpiece. The usual slow-running horizontal-single lived under the floor, dominated by an outsize flywheel, steering was by tiller, and final drive by central chain. A concession to the horseless image was the dummy hood, and the radiator was said to contain no fewer than 314 tubes. Top speed was 25 m.p.h. This worthy ancestor of America's first modern 'compact' sold for $850 in its homeland.

## FORD MODEL-A, 1903

The first production Ford could easily be mistaken for a Cadillac—the traditional under-floor engine cranked from the side, there was the same two-speed planetary gearbox, and final drive was by a central chain. The wheel steering and nose-piece housing a recessed tubular cooler heightened the resemblance. Only a year before this car was made, the two Henrys (Ford and Leland) had parted company, allegedly because Ford felt that racing improved the breed, whereas Leland did not. Both erstwhile partners prospered, but on 1903 form even the most intelligent prophet could not have foretold the shape of things to come. The Ford was a bigger and heavier car with two cylinders to the Cadillac's one, and it cost $100 more. Both factories sold some 1,700 cars during their first full season of manufacture.

## RENAULT 8 H.P., 1903

By the turn of the century Louis Renault's *voiturettes* were firmly established. Like de Dion-Bouton, he preferred shafts to belts or chains, and his sliding-type box incorporated a direct top gear. Inevitably the young firm started to make its own engines, this 1·7-litre vertical-twin being the work of Viet, whom Renault had enticed away from de Dion. As yet automatic inlet valves were retained, and the classic coal-shovel bonnet was flanked by twin lateral radiators. But also in evidence was the genesis of the *marque's* Edwardian reputation as a simple and reliable town carriage. A mere five years later 1,100 c.c. of Billancourt's stolid, imperturbable horses would be carting *carrosserie* of similar style and weight around the capitals of Europe.

## DE DION-BOUTON 8 H.P., 1904

Here is Europe's most universal and widely-copied light car of the period. The recipe—a simple 942 c.c. high-speed single-cylinder engine, a fool-proof constant-mesh box, easy lubrication by a three-way hand pump, and the celebrated de Dion drive, dispensing with breakable chains or slip-prone belts. And all this with tonneau coachwork, thanks to M. le Marquis de Dion and M. Georges Bouton. By 1902 the engine lived at the front end, and though the pedal-operated decelerator still allowed one to 'step off the gas', so to speak, a third forward ratio rendered control a trifle more complicated. Bottom was pre-selected by foot, the column shift took care of second and top, and a side lever selected reverse. Puteaux were talking in terms of 200 cars a month by the end of 1901, and even if this was wishful thinking, the number of survivors to be seen today speaks for itself.

## DELAUGÈRE, 1904

Appearances can deceive. The replica raceabout coachwork suggests a 1905 Gordon Bennett de Dietrich, but the Delaugère from Orléans was about as unsporting a *marque* as ever saw the light of day, its impact being regional rather than national, and its specification copybook, apart from an abortive flirtation with slide valves in 1913. Already in 1904 the Panhard idiom was acquiring Mercédès overtones, and the radiator tubes were confined within a shell, though side chains were still the safest way of transmitting power from a large four-cylinder engine to the rear wheels. Not that even small firms were immune from brute force for brute force's sake: the biggest of the 1905 crop of Delaugères disposed of 15-odd litres.

## LAGONDA, 1905

Made by an American opera singer on the banks of the Thames, the Lagonda's reputation was still confined to the ranks of graduate motor-cyclists. Understandably, for the tricar was not a particularly civilised mode of transportation. Its motorbike ancestry apart, it was unsociable and exposed its passenger to dust and incidents alike. But women were women then, and their escorts benefited from a good power-to-weight ratio at low first cost. Early examples had little of the car in their make-up but there are traces of sophistication in the Lagonda's water-cooled vee-twin engine, wheel steering, and rather uncertain brakes at front and rear. The tricar's vogue was ephemeral: sidecars had been invented in 1902, and five years later the breed was moribund.

## CADILLAC MODEL-M, 1906

In America, the big and woolly underfloor-mounted 'single' and planetary gearbox were still with us in 1906, but European influences reflected themselves in the abbreviated bonnet full of nothing, the water tank apart. Cadillac's 12-litre i.o.e. unit developed 10 b.h.p. at a gentle 750 r.p.m., though one wonders how any horses escaped via the huge silencer, rightly termed a muffler in its country of origin. This four-seater on a 6 ft. 4 in. wheelbase was capable of 30 m.p.h., and cost $1,100 (lamps extra). Primitive the Cadillac might be, but the Dewar Trophy award for the famous standardisation test of 1908 was a significant pointer, especially at a time when wise motorists invested in screw-cutting lathes to cope with replacement parts that didn't fit!

## FORD MODEL-N, 1906

The Ford was taking shape. Its transverse suspension was a desirable feature on America's bad roads, and Henry's obstinacy was to ensure that it outlived him. Two-speed, pedal-controlled planetary transmissions were still standard wear in the runabout class, but Ford stole a march on his rivals by adopting a front-mounted vertical four-cylinder engine in place of the old horizontal singles and twins, not to mention shaft drive. A weight of only 700 lb. meant a top speed of 40 m.p.h., far beyond an Oldsmobile's capabilities. To add insult to injury, Model-N undercut the price of the cheapest Olds by $50. Henry Ford's advertising might still claim that he was the world's largest maker of 'sixes', but he was fast learning the recipe for success.

## RENAULT AX-TYPE, 1907

If one were asked to name the commonest European Veteran, the answer would surely be the ubiquitous 9 h.p. Renault first seen in 1905, and attaining its brief moment of immortality nine years later in long-chassis form as *le taxi de la Marne*. Specification was, of course, classic Renault with big dashboard radiator, three-speed box, direct top gear, bevel drive, and the awkward (but still widely used) quadrant change. The 1,100 c.c. vertical-twin engine often had to work hard in competition with the weight of its elegant coachwork, and the cabs really were overbodied, but the 'AX' was good for 35 m.p.h. and would chug inexorably up hill and down dale, all at a frugal 35 m.p.g.

## DELAHAYE, 1909

The presence of a neat and modest monobloc four-cylinder engine under a modern bonnet line sorts ill with the surrey coachwork (complete with fringe), solid rubber on the wheels, and side-chain drive, but this is a *camionnette* made by a firm always more interested in trucks than private cars. At the 1908 Paris Salon they displayed no fewer than 13 examples, ranging from lightweights with their new 12-16 h.p. engine up to vast fire-engines. Not that all Delahayes were rustic: those who were startled when the redoubtable Charles Weiffenbach launched his Type-135 sports car in 1935 should have remembered that the 8-litre chain-driven model of 1906 was an early favourite of that motoring monarch, Alfonso XIII of Spain.

## BRASIER '12-18', 1910

Once the cars from Ivry-Port had carried off two Gordon Bennett Cups, had earned Léon Théry his nickname of 'Chronometer', and had enjoyed the patronage of young bloods—not to mention their uncles and aunts. Alas, the slump of 1907 took its toll, and many a factory discovered that even in a world of cheap labour the answer was not a vast range embracing everything from a twin-cylinder cab chassis to 10-odd litres of chain-driven 'six' with a nice line in crankshaft whip. Between these two extremes there was generally a serviceable monobloc 'four' with four forward speeds and shaft drive: the Brasier version ran to 1,847 c.c. and would do 42 m.p.h. Almost the only surviving trace of Homburg and Clermont-Ferrand was the shouldered radiator—M. Brasier was, like Schmidt of Packard and Terrasse of Hotchkiss, an old Mors hand.

## DE DION-BOUTON 14 H.P., 1910

Success breeds respectability, and respectability turns, all too easily, to dullness. De Dions in the early 1900s were simple, individual, and excellent value for money: by 1910 the famous final-drive arrangements were found on some models only, the radiator was ordinary, and the only unusual feature of the three-speed gearbox was its difficult vertical-gate change. If de Dion's pressure lubrication still lifted it out of the ruck, the cylinders of the 2·1-litre engine were cast in pairs at a time when monobloc power units were coming into fashion, and, unlike the 'singles', the 14 h.p. was no outstanding bargain. Therein lay the rub, and though de Dion were still prosperous to the extent of launching an ambitious range of big vee-eights, the writing was on the wall.

## DELAUNAY-BELLEVILLE 'HB.4', 1911

No owner ever took the wheel: yet Nicholas II of Russia, President Poincaré, and many a lesser potentate rode behind the gracefully rounded radiator, a reminder that the same factory had made the boilers for H.M. Yacht *Victoria and Albert*. Some of Saint-Denis's more florid copy was the work of Anatole France and Edmond Rostand—no less. Further, the 'Car Magnificent' was also a 'car civilised', with comprehensive undertray and full-pressure lubrication. As befitted the best type of town carriage, the Delaunay-Belleville was more often found in six-cylinder form, but there were some 'fours', this one disposing of 3·7 litres, side valves, and a four-speed gearbox. The firm never recovered from World War I, and the vee-radiators of 1919 models presaged a slow decline terminating in a crypto-Mercedes speaking halting English.

## PANHARD X.7, 1911

Panhard et Levassor had once been the world's exemplars, but by 1911 little of moment was happening in the Avenue d'Ivry. Radiators were redolent of 1904, pressed-steel frames were relatively recent arrivals on the scene, and not even the adoption of the Silent, if smoky, Knight engine seemed likely to ripple the stagnating surface. Not that the old firm was moribund—it had another 28 years of sleeve-valvery in front of it, and some of the big Panhard-Knights with the 'double-S' badge were *grand'routiers* in the best French tradition. For that matter, the X.7 was no sluggard: 42 b.h.p. were extracted from 4.4 litres and four cylinders, sufficient to propel open cars at 60 m.p.h. There were four forward speeds, while surprisingly Panhard arranged both foot and hand brakes to work on the rear wheels.

## ROLLS-ROYCE 'SILVER GHOST', 1911

In any company the Rolls-Royce cannot be ignored. Would-be detractors poke fun at the messy underbonnet vista, and remind us that 48 b.h.p. from 7-plus litres were no great shakes in 1906, let alone in 1911, when the 'Ghost' had really 'arrived'. But the model won its spurs, not on what it did, but on how, and for how long, it went on doing it. In any case a silent and effortless 60 m.p.h. was adequate for the roads and police-traps of the day, and with reasonable bodywork 15 m.p.g. represented a frugality we have long since ceased to expect from the elephantine. Those who lay bets on the auction prices of Edwardian Rolls-Royces may note that this one was *walled up* in 1930 by a disgruntled owner reluctant to accept a risible offer. It did not emerge from immurement for 30 years.

## CHENARD-WALCKER, 1912

To the casual observer only a handsome oval radiator redeemed the Chenard-Walcker from the stereotype of the period—side-valve monobloc four-cylinder engine, magneto ignition, four-speed gearbox, and pedestrian coachwork. The Touté-designed o.h.c. sports cars were a thing of the future: as yet the firm did not race. But beneath the surface there was the ingenious double-reduction drive, with bevel gears and differential mounted on top of the dead rear axle, and imparting motion via half-shafts to small pinions meshing with internally-toothed drums on the rear wheels. The system was both quiet and durable. Chenards came in 2-litre, 2·6-litre and 3-litre sizes, the biggest Type-U recording a respectable 56 m.p.h. and 27 m.p.g. when tested by a leading motor journal in 1912.

## CLÉMENT-BAYARD 12 H.P., 1912

In 1912 dashboard radiators were no longer the prerogative of Renault—they could be seen on many a breed, including Charrons from France, Arrol-Johnstons from Scotland, Komnicks from Germany, and Keetons from America. The Clément-Bayard's ancestry was deep-rooted and complex, even if by this time the principal hallmark of Adolphe Clément's creations was the emblem of his hero, the Chevalier Bayard, emblazoned upon the blunt coal-shovel nose of this orthodox and pedestrian small 'four'. After 1918 the firm, like Charron and Arrol-Johnston, moved their cooling arrangements up front, but stolid respectability was no longer sufficient to sell cars. The Clément-Bayard was dead by 1922.

## HUPMOBILE '32', 1912

When the Model-T Ford took its bow in 1908, it was by no means *hors concours*. The first Hupmobile appeared only a few months afterwards, and was an altogether smaller affair with pair-cast cylinders and conventional sliding-type gearbox. As this offered only two very widely-spaced ratios it was not much improvement on the Ford's pedal-controlled system, but the Hupp was a racy-looking little car with less than two litres under the bonnet, and an abbreviated wheelbase. By 1912 this had been stretched within and without to 2·8 litres, while a longer chassis allowed for full four-seater coachwork. There was also a much-needed intermediate cog, all of which helped the company to sell over 12,000 cars in 1913, and to continue their popular 'four' until 1925.

## MAXWELL 'MESSENGER', 1912

Here is another traditional American two-speeder. As late as 1910 not a few makers still preferred a big flat-twin to a 'four', even if they now mounted it up front under a bonnet. The popular Maxwell's engine boasted oversquare dimensions and magneto ignition, and final drive was by shaft, though the full-elliptic springs struck an archaic note. Doors were an innovation on a cheap lightweight: Ford's 'fore-door' touring meant just that. This handy little runabout cost $625 in its native land, or £150 in London. Unfortunately the *marque*'s sponsors overreached themselves, and though the Maxwell survived the collapse of the parent United States Motor Company, it continued as an undistinguished if inexpensive 'four' on orthodox lines until the Chrysler takeover in the early 1920s.

## NAPIER 15 H.P., 1912

The Napier could still be mentioned in the same breath as Rolls-Royce, thanks to S. F. Edge's early racing successes, and his tireless advocacy of the six-cylinder engine. Inevitably the four-cylinder cars were played down, but nevertheless they remained Acton's bread-and-butter, and in 'Extra Strong Colonial' form they earned their keep in such unlikely places as South America. The 2·7-litre side-valve engine had pair-cast cylinders, three forward speeds were deemed sufficient, and final drive was by worm. At less that £400 for a chassis it was good value. Unfortunately the nabobs who rode in the lordly Forty-Fives and Sixties didn't like to see the 'water-tower' filler cap on taxicabs. . . .

## BERLIET 25 H.P., 1913

The Berliet's locomotive emblem is symbolic of a firm which now concentrates on heavy commercial vehicles. In 40-odd years of private-car manufacture they seldom deviated far from the norm, though the 1913 offering was well-made, not inelegant, and, in its larger manifestations, quite brisk as well, one of these '25s' winning fame at Brooklands motor course under the sobriquet of 'Whistling Rufus'. Under the bonnet was a straightforward s.v. monobloc 'four', the clutch was a multi-plate, and there were four forward speeds, not to mention the option of electric lights and starter. This example depicts the station wagon's snobbish ancestor, equally at home transporting guns to the butts, or servants to the village 'hop'. The presence of a canework moulding suggests that the former use was paramount.

## CADILLAC 20-30 H.P., 1913

By the outbreak of World War I the Cadillac was emerging as 'the Standard of the World' in more ways than one. Since 1906 the range had included a big four-cylinder model with separately cast cylinders and copper water jacketing, and this $5\frac{1}{2}$-litre machine was quite a performer, with 60 m.p.h. on tap. In 1912 it acquired Charles F. Kettering's ingenious electric starter, and within two years all but its cheapest compatriots had fallen into line. 1914 Cadillacs had two-speed back axles, nearly 20 years before the advent of Auburn's famed 'dual ratio' arrangement, and 1915 saw the first commercially successful vee-eight, though this time Cadillac were chronologically well behind de Dion-Bouton of France. Streamlining is already in evidence, with the side-laps half concealed in the scuttle: on contemporary Ramblers they were completely faired-in.

## HUDSON '37', 1913

When the Hudson first lost its identity in the 1950s, and then vanished altogether in the cut-throat competition of the American automobile industry, it left many mourners in Europe. Starting as a modest four-cylinder affair in 1909, the *marque* made its great impact with the 'Super Six' of 1916, and consolidated this with the well-loved Eights of 1930 onward. This '37' was the last of the 'fours' and typifies contemporary American thinking: there are still some vestiges of the horseless-carriage configuration, but already electrics are present. By contrast with their modern counterparts, Detroit's 1913 wares tended to look smaller than they actually were. The Hudson's wheelbase was a respectable 9 ft. 10 in., and there were more than $4\frac{1}{2}$ litres of side-valve engine.

## PEUGEOT '14-20', 1913

In pre-1914 days a big manufacturer such as Peugeot offered an immensely complicated range, and the contemporary catalogue ran to five basic types and limitless sub-variants, from the unorthodox Bugatti-designed 'Bébé' to a hefty $7\frac{1}{2}$-litre '40-50', with four large 'pots' disposing of a useful 92 b.h.p. Altogether more modest was this 2·8-litre '14-20', yet another European family tourer in the traditional mould—four cylinders, four forward speeds, and room for commodious coachwork on a wheelbase of 10 ft. 6 in. Unusual for the period were the underslung worm drive and a footbrake working on the rear wheels, when a large drum behind the gearbox was still routine wear. Wire wheels were an optional extra, and with Peugeot's competition career at its zenith nobody worried much about the modest 32 brake horses found beneath the well-proportioned bonnet.

## A.C. 'SOCIABLE', 1914

The period 1911-14 represents the zenith of the cyclecar boom, but the concept had never died out, even after the demise of the tricar, and the A.C. 'Sociable' was one of the missing links. Based on a three-wheeled parcelcar introduced in 1907, it was powered by a 700 c.c. side-valve single-cylinder engine mounted ahead of the rear wheel, which it drove via a pedal-controlled two-speed epicyclic gear. More engaging was the tiller, which moved in a horizontal plane: on full left lock it could butt the conductor playfully in the stomach. Hood and screen were extras, as were horn, speedometer, and brakes on the front wheels. Maximum speed was 25 m.p.h., but the A.C. could put up quite a good average on long runs. It did not survive World War I.

## BENZ 18-45 PS, 1914

Karl Benz's conservative phase was over by 1902, when the primitive 'Velo' disappeared from the catalogue for good. By 1914 the firm's reputation was founded on a series of fast tourers of solid construction: these embraced everything from the little 2-litre '8-20' up to 10 litres of 39-100 PS, now with shaft drive in place of the side chains of earlier giants. Bigger cars had pair-cast cylinders, and the 4·7-litre '18-45' came halfway up the range. A prominent feature is the *Spitzkühler*, hallmark of sporting machinery from Germany. After World War I this fashion spread to even the stodgiest species, though the norm for a German manufacturer was a 2½-litre side-valve tourer of immense weight, generally with a lethargic performance and a foot transmission brake.

## LOCOMOBILE '48', 1914

Many of America's's great cars were seldom seen in Europe. The Locomobile '48' was available in 1911, and it was still in the catalogue when the *marque* (by now William C. Durant's prestige line) vanished for good in 1929. By this time it was a museum piece, with its 9-litre T-headed six-cylinder engine and vast radiator suggestive of an Edwardian Mercedes. Admittedly it had acquired four-wheel brakes, and coil ignition had supplanted the dual magnetos of earlier days, but it was still a lot of car weighing a good 2½ tons, and costing around $12,000. Its 1914 counterpart was rather cheaper, though already endowed with full electrics, while the 'gunboat roadster' bodywork on this example would not have looked out of place a decade later.

## METZ '25', 1915

American styling had lapsed into uniformity by 1915, but beneath the surface all was not always what it seemed to be. The Metz was singular both in background and design. Its friction-and-chain drive offering an infinite number of ratios was unexpected on so large a vehicle: further, the *marque*'s antecedents included a primordial kit-car, sold in 14 packages at $25 a time. Yet Charles Metz's venture prospered to the tune of victory in the 1913 Glidden Tour, which persuaced him to remain loyal to his peculiar transmission until America's entry into the war. For the rest, the Metz was a conventional s.v. 'four' of just over three litres' capacity. Full electrics formed part of an ensemble that cost only $600, f.o.b. Waltham, Massachusetts.

## PACKARD '3-38', 1915

Of the famous 'three Ps of America', Packard survived the longest, and commands a fanatical following to this day. Their first European-type car, the Model-L of 1904, was said to be a crib of the Mors, but it introduced a radiator shape which remained unaltered for 28 years. 1911 saw the company's first 'six', the 7-litre '48' with pair-cast cylinders, and this line of development was pursued until 1915. Body lines might be conservative, but beneath the surface the Packard was quite advanced. Full electrics were of course mandatory by this time in Detroit; unexpected were the spiral bevel final drive and dipping headlights. If the crowned heads of Europe had yet to discover the Packard, the connoisseur with $3,750 to hand had no need to do his shopping in the importers' showrooms of Manhattan.

## CHEVROLET '490', 1916

If their 1929 six-cylinder gave Chevrolet the edge over Ford in the American sales race, it was the '490' that provided them with a weapon against Lizzie. By 1916 the good old two-speed planetary box was getting a little long in the tooth, and the Chevrolet's orthodox three-speed gear-set and overhead-valve engine (with exposed pushrods) represented quite an advance on Model-T. Springing was by quarter-elliptics all round, and there was no handbrake, the 'service' system being operated by the clutch pedal, while the foot-operated 'emergency' brake incorporated a ratchet for parking. The model designation represented the list price in dollars, though electric lighting and starting set you back another $60. Sales quadrupled in six years: General Motors, who took over in 1917, had bought themselves a gold mine.

## DETROIT ELECTRIC, 1917

The battery-electric car is returning to favour in these days of congested streets, but its first incarnation was really over by 1910, when the limitations of range and performance restricted its clientele to conservative carriage folk with a penchant for afternoon visiting. Such people cared naught for style, and there was nothing in the machinery to wear out: hence sales were low, and the 'china-closet' bodywork and bar steering persisted to the end. Both hood and boot served as repositories for the accumulators, and as late as 1941 it was still possible to buy a Detroit Electric. Some of the last ones combined the angular *carrosserie* with front ends lifted from Willys or Dodge, but this only served to destroy the old baroque charm.

## STANLEY '735', 1917

Even as late as the 1920s steam still had its loyal adherents amongst those who appreciated smoothness, silence, and neck-snapping acceleration, and were prepared to put up with slow cold-morning starts—50 minutes from scratch—and a certain inherent breathlessness which meant that a sprint up a long hill was followed by a subsequent spell of *pianissimo*. Stanley boilers worked at 55 p.s.i., while water consumption improved considerably after the adoption of a condenser in 1915: this masqueraded in various styles as a 'radiator', the Mercedes *Spitzkühler* being favoured in 1917. The engine was geared direct to the back axle, and a wooden frame was used. The wire wheels on this example have been cut down to take modern tyres.

## PACKARD 'TWIN-SIX', 1918

One sure road to greater flexibility and silence was a multiplicity of cylinders, and hot on the heels of Cadillac's 1915 vee-eight came seven litres of V-12 by Packard in 1916. Output was a staid 88 b.h.p., but prices started at $2,600, which was not a lot of money. The 'Twin-Six' was the first American touring car with aluminium pistons. It also had a curious control layout—left-hand drive with left-hand levers—but the conventional American configuration was adopted with the Second Series of 1917. At the same time cylinder heads were made detachable, and bonnet and body acquired a 'stream line'. Customers included Tsar Nicholas II, President Warren G. Harding, and at least one Chinese War Lord. The model was produced until 1923.

## DARMONT-MORGAN, 1921

H. F. S. Morgan's three-wheeler for graduate motorcyclists had a 40-year span of life. The formula was simple—a tubular frame with central backbone, coil-spring and sliding-pillar i.f.s., and a two-speed chain-transmission. The big vee-twin motorcycle engine, initially by J.A.P., lived out of doors and cranked from the side. Electric lighting was not optional until 1921, starters (which in any case could not cope) came later, and only in the 1930s could one buy a Morgan that would go backwards. Coupled brakes and foot accelerators were never provided on the 'twins'. The end-product lacked creature comforts and demanded considerable skill from its operator, but it had plenty of urge. This example was built under licence by Darmont in France.

## FORD MODEL-T, 1921

A wintry landscape for the Universal Car of all time, perhaps rivalled only by the Volkswagen. Henry Ford's Tin Lizzie was ubiquitous: it would go anywhere, could be maintained by those innocent of mechanical skill, and could also be driven by them, provided they remembered certain 'simple little rules and few'—otherwise the pedal-controlled two-speed transmission could play a trick or two. By 1921 the all-round transverse springing, tiny and ineffectual brakes, and high, boxy coachwork were showing their age, while the Ford had lost most of its charm in 1917, when the uncompromising black of paint and upholstery were matched by a pedestrian radiator with black shell. This is the 'Center Door' sedan: one door per passenger was not to be the order of the day at Dearborn until 1923.

## MINERVA 30CV, 1921

The 'Goddess of Automobiles' is one of the neglected Classics of Europe, though it typifies Belgian automobile engineering at its zenith. Minerva was a great name in the motorcycling world before progressing to cars, and the *marque*'s reputation lasted well into the 1930s. From 1909 the Knight double-sleeve-valve engine was standardised, and some of their bigger models—notably the 6-litre 'AKS' of 1929 with light steel sleeves—could perform impressively. The image, however, remained the same: a four-square, chauffeur-driven carriage, spiritual successor to France's Delaunay-Belleville in pre-war years. Minerva made a good recovery from the German occupation, and typical of their post-war offerings is this 5·3-litre 'six' with separate four-speed gearbox, magneto ignition, cone clutch, and brakes on the rear wheels only.

## CITROEN 5CV, 1922

André Citroën introduced mass-production methods to France in 1919, and from his original A-type stemmed the 5CV of 1921, a stolid little vehicle with 856 c.c. four-cylinder engine developing 11 b.h.p. The disc wheels, lemon-yellow paintwork, and pointed-tail cloverleaf bodywork conferred an individuality which the specification lacked, and the foot-brake worked, none too well, on the transmission. Front-wheel brakes were never offered, even at the end of the model's run in 1926, but the *cinq chevaux* ground inexorably along at 35 m.p.h., and continued to do so in the backwoods of France until quite recently. Opel copied the design in Germany, and an attempt was made in 1928 to bring the design up to date as the Sima-Standard. It did not prosper—only Citroën could make a Citroën.

## PIERCE-ARROW, 1922

To the bitter end in 1938, Pierce-Arrow stood apart. Both style and publicity were conservative, and they built big, usually with headlamps faired into the front wings. In the later 'teens, the range was headed by the '66', some 13 litres of T-headed 'six' with room to walk about inside, but the Vintage Twin Valve Six, though big enough in all conscience, was a mere seven-litre tiddler on an 11 ft. 6 in. wheelbase. The old-fashioned engine apart, specification was conventional, and the design persisted until 1928, when the Buffalo firm came up with a more modern straight-eight, followed three seasons later by an even more magnificent V-12. This example was acquired in decrepit condition at the 1962 Sword Sale at Balgray.

## HOTCHKISS 'AM', 1923

Hotchkiss's slogan was *le juste milieu,* and after 1918 their speciality was an upper-middle-class tourer of some quality, but with a minimum of frills. The presence of an Englishman, Harry Ainsworth, at the helm at Saint-Denis prevented any unnecessary exuberance, but the Hotchkiss, if a trifle unrefined by contrast with Delage or Darracq, was something of a performer, especially in later six-cylinder, $3\frac{1}{2}$-litre form. In the 1920s, however, they concentrated on 'fours', the 'AM' having a 2·4-litre side-valve engine of conventional design, four-wheel brakes, a disc clutch, and four forward speeds. The angular Weymann saloon body typifies French styling in the period: later 'AMs' had overhead valves, spear-heading a whole generation of big 'fours', that continued until the end of private-car production in 1954.

## BALLOT 2LT, 1924

Ernest Ballot made proprietary engines and racing cars before he made tourers in series, and the 2LT was one of that splendid family of fast 2-litre machinery (others were Théophile Schneider, O.M. and Lagonda) which enlivened the 1920s. Features were a four-cylinder engine with gear-driven o.h.c., four-wheel brakes, and a four-speed box with positive central change, and the cars were often seen with square-rigged fabric saloon coachwork by Van Vooren. Sports versions would top the 70 mark, and the breed persisted until 1928, before giving way to some less distinguished straight-eights. The *coupé de ville* body seems rather a burden for such a sportive chassis, but it must be remembered that what was 'sports' to the English-speaking world was often nothing of the sort on the Continent.

## LORRAINE-DIETRICH 15CV, 1924

Ignore the handsome radiator, and the detachable steel wheels, and you might take this for a better-class American assembled tourer of the early 1920s, instead of the illustrious scion of an illustrious French house— Lorraine-Dietrich of Argenteuil. Left-hand drive, a three-speed gear-box, and central change were slightly non-U in 1919, and the exposed pushrods of the valve gear smacked of Chevrolet as well. None the less, the 'Silken Six' had a long innings—1920 to 1932— and it won at Le Mans twice in succession, in 1925 and 1926. Later cars had four forward speeds, but it was effectively the swansong both of the *marque* and of designer Marius Barbarou. Argenteuil took the final curtain in 1934, with a species of Gallic Humber 'Snipe', even down to the side valves.

## CHEVROLET 'SUPERIOR' MODEL-K, 1925

Chevrolet were moving up fast in 1925. Not that the standard article, here seen in roadster form, was any more inspiring to the eye than the original '490'—probably less so. There were still no brakes on the front wheels, only the rims were detachable, the valve gear lived out of doors as in 1916, and lubrication was strictly splash. On the credit side, the semi-elliptic suspension gave a less bouncy ride, while with a capacity of 2·8 litres and a wheelbase of 8 ft. 7 in., the 'Superior' was a real compact. In any case, the proof of the pudding is in the eating, and sales of half a million cars indicated clearly that the new Chevrolet was what the public in America—and many other countries—wanted.

## DE DION-BOUTON 'IT', 1925

One could still buy a de Dion-Bouton in 1925—or, for that matter, in 1932—but *marque*-loyalty was the only legitimate reason for such a purchase. Gone was the elegant simplicity of the 'singles', and even the ambitious if not wholly successful vee-eight had departed from the catalogue, as had the de Dion axle. What one got was a stodgy piece of Vintage-perpendicular, hard to distinguish from a Unic or a La Licorne. Admittedly there were brakes on all four wheels, but deviations from the norm symbolised decline rather than progressive thought—cantilever rear suspension and a fixed cylinder head. The 1,847 c.c. side-valve four-cylinder engine developed a mere 25 b.h.p. A creeping atrophy had descended on Puteaux.

## FIAT '501', 1925

Italy has originated many a fashion in bodywork, but the nation's stock offerings inclined towards the imitative, and pear-shaped radiators were the recognised trans-Alpine wear from 1913 to the early 1920s. Symbolic of the era was the first mass-production Fiat, the '501' introduced in 1919. Its durability and sewing-machine smoothness were much appreciated, but it was relatively expensive, and in original form with anchors on the rear wheels only it did not stop very well, perhaps because for once its makers eschewed the transmission brake, a hallmark of the breed until the 1960s. The $1\frac{1}{2}$-litre s.v. four-cylinder engine gave a staid 18 b.h.p., the four-speed gearbox was obviously intended for assaults on the vertical, and 45-50 m.p.h. was about the limit.

## MERCEDES MODEL-K, 1925

If the origins of Untertürkheim's golden age of *donner und blitzen* were far from humble, they were not exactly inspired, either, and the Model-K's reputation was infelicitous. Signs of a brighter future were detectable in the big 6·2-litre overhead-camshaft engine, the vane-type blower engaged by a second pressure on the loud pedal, the exhaust pipes sprouting from the bonnet side, and the aggressive vee-radiator, shortly to be banished from lesser brands of Mercedes: but the 'K', though good for more than 90 m.p.h. thanks to the 160 b.h.p. furnished by the *Kompressor*, was weak on brakes and roadholding. This formal cabriolet was executed by the Berlin coachbuilders Erdmann and Rossi for the actor Emil Jannings.

## RENAULT 40CV, 1925

The elephantine will always have its allure, and though the biggest Renault was outmoded by 1925, it was still a lot of car for its price. The 9,123 c.c. bi-block six-cylinder s.v. engine had fixed heads, 'long' versions measured 13 ft. 1½in. between wheel centres, and tourers turned the scales at 2½ tons. It carried 25 gallons of fuel, two of oil, and no less than 12 of water in the vast dashboard radiator, and at a respectable 2,700 r.p.m. the unit developed 140 b.h.p., enough for a performance that could be lethal even with the four-wheel brakes introduced in 1922. A stripped '40' was the first car to average over 100 m.p.h. for 24 hours, but the model is best remembered as the carriage of French Presidents in the 1920s.

## LANCIA 'LAMBDA', 1926

Advanced from any standpoint, the 'Lambda' was a touring car that could take on all manner of sporting machinery on handling alone. If the unitary construction of chassis and body were abandoned in later years at the behest of the coachbuilders, the so-called 'sliding-pillar' i.f.s. remained, while Lancia's compact narrow-angle o.h.c. vee-four engine left plenty of room for the most prolific Italian families. What is more, this impressive specification was introduced in 1922. A third place in the 1928 Mille Miglia represented the peak of a limited competition career, but latter-day enthusiasts have 'cut and shut' these elongated cars, not always with the happiest of results. The cycle-type wings on this factory-built torpedo suggest that someone has been 'having a go' on a rather less drastic scale.

## PACKARD 'SUPER EIGHT', 1927

The American doctrine of yearly model changes had little or no effect on the Packard. In 1923 the 'Twin-Six' gave way to a splendid nine-bearing straight-eight with four-wheel brakes, and this was produced almost until Pearl Harbour. The shape hardly changed at all before 1932, when a vee-radiator was adopted. Technically the 1927s are significant as the first to use hypoid final drive, but the drum-shaped headlamps (a mid-Vintage fad) are an easier dating feature from the outside. With 80 m.p.h. available from the smooth and flexible 6·3-litre power unit, one need not wonder that such diametrically-opposed heads of state as Josef Stalin and King Alexander of Yugoslavia were partial to the breed.

## FIAT '520', 1928

By the later 1920s European six-cylinder family cars were aping America in engineering and style alike: not a bad idea, since America had much of the know-how in this field. The 2¼-litre side-valve Fiat with its coil ignition, boxy lines, artillery wheels, and mock-Rolls-Royce radiator, was no oil painting, and flat out at 60 m.p.h., but it had a useful four-speed gearbox, and sold well in England. These seven-bearing 'sixes' were the first Fiats with l.h.d., and the design survived until 1936. The later ones with dual-circuit hydraulic brakes and raised compression were quite fun to drive, and the sports models were pretty into the bargain.

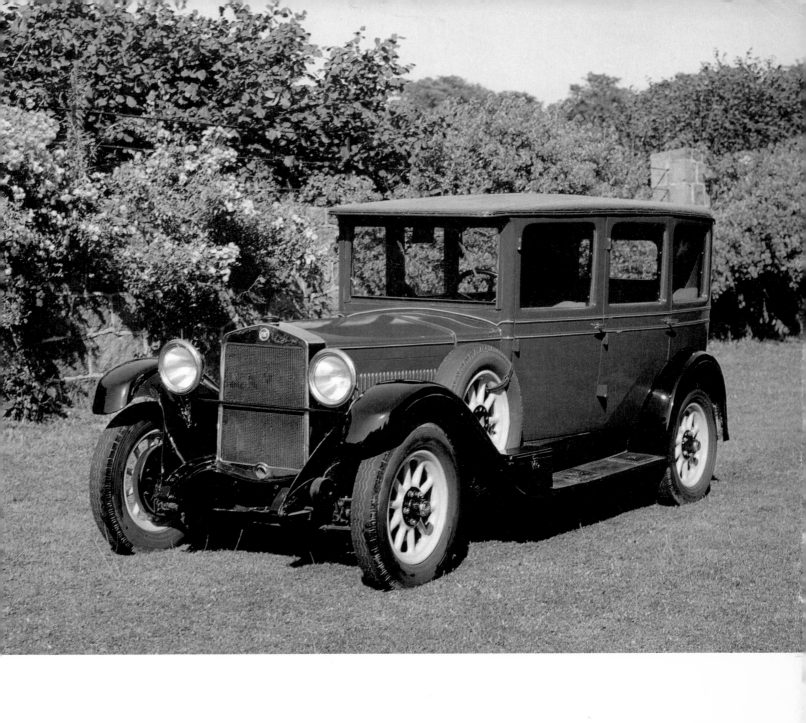

## FRANKLIN, 1928

Franklin had been turning out air-cooled cars in Syracuse, N.Y., for 27 years when this 3·9-litre 'Airman' sedan was made, and they had another six years of individuality in front of them. Admittedly, some idiosyncrasies had been jettisoned by 1928: de Causse's handsome mock-radiator had replaced the ugly horse-collar air intake, and four-wheel hydraulic brakes had made their appearance, but still in evidence were the full-elliptic springs, which gave an excellent ride on rough surfaces. Only the short-wheelbase cars retained the wooden frame. If 65 m.p.h. was as fast as one could go, the Franklin could not be mistaken for anything else, and its adherents included flyers like Charles Lindbergh and Amelia Earhart.

## OPEL 4/18 PS, 1928

Germany took a long time to recover from the effects of World War I, and it was not until 1935 that Opel, the country's largest manufacturer, managed to deliver 100,000 vehicles in a single season. Though General Motors only moved in in 1929, American influence is already apparent in the miniature-Chevrolet look. Specification was entirely orthodox—a two-bearing 1-litre side-valve engine, 6-volt coil ignition, three forward speeds, and mechanical brakes, while the quarter-elliptic springs were a heritage from the car's Citroën-based ancestor, the 'Laubfrosch'. The Opel was a dull car in a dull period, but it helped to give Rüsselsheim 40 per cent of the home market, not to mention nearly 30 per cent of the nation's export sales.

## STUTZ 'BB', 1928

The Indianapolis-built Stutz might be short on glamour, and the company's finances might dictate adherence to a proven straight-eight while the American carriage trade plunged headlong into the multi-barrelled engine, but this o.h.c. model with hydraulic brakes and worm drive was not only fast—it could and did give the Bentleys a good run for their money at Le Mans in 1928, running the $4\frac{1}{2}$-litre very close. The 'BB' offered 115 b.h.p. in standard form, equal to a road speed of about 90 m.p.h.: this 1928 model, exceptionally, wears wood wheels and detachable rims in place of the wire type usually found. Also atypical is the coachbuilt tourer bodywork, for Stutz (almost alone among American makers) were addicted to Weymann's system of fabric construction.

## BUGATTI TYPE 46, 1929

A town carriage from Molsheim? Surely here we have a contradiction in terms. But no—Ettore could and did achieve this objective with the 5·3-litre Type 46, a single o.h.c. straight-eight in the best tradition, with three valves per cylinder and one of those splendidly sculptured blocks. A contemporary report credited it with 'the luxury of a limousine, the flexibility and top-gear performance of a thoroughbred town carriage, and the perfect road-holding, speed and acceleration of the best type of sports model': and it would see 90 m.p.h. in saloon form. In effect it was a scaled-down 'Royale', which accounts for a three-speed gearbox mounted in unit with the rear axle. Nobody missed the extra ratio, but the arrangement made life difficult for the home mechanic. Type 46 was still catalogued in 1939.

## FORD MODEL-A, 1929

The best substitute for a Universal Car is another universal car, and Model-A inherited most of Model-T's virtues—simplicity, ease of driving, a high ground clearance, and a suspension capable of coping with the rough stuff—without any of Lizzie's infuriating idiosyncracies. Looks were obviously inspired by Henry Ford's prestige line, the Lincoln, and if the 3·3-litre side-valve engine had only four cylinders, then this was still true in 1928, not only of the Chevrolet, but also of Chrysler's new bargain-basement item, the Plymouth. Brakes might not be Model-A's forte, but it would see an honest 65 m.p.h., carried one of the world's first series-production station wagon bodies, and sold five million—this in spite of the fact that the Chevrolet was a 'six' from 1929 onwards.

## DAIMLER '35-120', 1930

Here is the dowager-image *in excelsis*, straight from the world of *Brideshead Revisited*: the ageless sleeve-valve Daimler, traditional transport of debutantes to the ball, and mourners to the cemetery. The owner seldom, if ever, drove it: thus it is surprising that by 1930 Daimler had adopted preselection and the fluid flywheel, devices which rendered the conduct of 2½ tons of stately carriage on a 13-foot wheelbase relatively painless. Despite the firm's preoccupation with vee-twelves renowned for extreme flexibility and gargantuan thirsts, this '35' was a 'six' powered by a vast and archaically untidy 5·8-litre seven-bearing engine. Typically Daimler were the worm-drive back axle, push-on handbrake lever, slatted shield over the fuel tank, and starter-button concealed under the floor carpet.

## RENAULT 'VIVASIX', 1930

There is no excuse for the veriest layman to mistake this big tourer for anything but a product of Billancourt, but beneath the traditional coal-shovel bonnet lurks heresy. The radiator now lives in front of the engine, and cooling is by pump instead of thermo-syphon. Otherwise little has changed, for side-by-side valves are retained, as are the American-type three-speed gearbox and transverse rear suspension which made for tricky handling on a fairly fast car capable of 65-70 m.p.h. The 'Vivasix' and its luxury version, the 'Vivastella', had a 3·2-litre six-cylinder engine and looked their best with open coachwork. Around 1935, alas, styling degenerated into a parody of Detroit.

## D.K.W. F-1500, 1931

In the early 1930s Germany shook off the atrophy of the previous decade, and became a forcing-house for advanced design. All-round independent suspension and front-wheel drive came to the fore, and most successful of the f.w.d. designs was J. S. Rasmussen's D.K.W., product of a firm renowned for its two-stroke motorcycles. The water-cooled twin-cylinder 500 c.c. engine lived athwart the chassis, ratios of the three-speed gearbox were selected by a handle on the dashboard, and a simple ladder-type frame kept weight down to 1,000 lb. Front suspension was by swinging half-axles. This early model had all-steel coachwork, but fabric was used on later types. Nearly 40,000 found buyers in 1937 alone, and descendants of the basic theme are still being made in the German Democratic Republic.

## HISPANO-SUIZA 54CV, 1932

If Midas fancied something big in 1932, he could still have it, from the drawing-board of Marc Birkigt at Bois-Colombes. $9\frac{1}{2}$ litres of pushrod V-12 engine with integral alloy heads, the usual lovely under-bonnet finish, four coils, and 24 sparking-plugs, developing 220 b.h.p. Chassis to choice—anything from a 'short' two-tonner up to a 13-footer for state occasions. In addition you can accelerate from 10 to 70 in top in around 20 seconds—far more esoteric. Not that you get all this for nothing, and £3,750 was a lot of money in 1932, even in Bond Street. Don't forget, either, that 54 French horses equal 75 of the sort understood by British or American tax-gatherers.

## ROLLS-ROYCE 'PHANTOM II', 1933

Even in 1933 'The Best Car in the World' had few rivals. If the bi-block 7.7-litre o.h.v. six-cylinder engine was a trifle old-fashioned in a generation of eights and twelves, all the old silence and flexibility were there. A hypoid rear axle kept even the most formal of limousines reasonably low, while the delectable four-speed gearbox now had synchromesh: Rolls-Royce were, in fact, the first all-British firm to adopt this refinement. A 'Phantom II' with closed coachwork would see 85-90 m.p.h., and the rare and desirable 'Continentals' were even faster, with the 'ton' available on a good road. Not that all this was cheap: Thrupp and Maberly asked £2,600 and more for a smart sedanca such as this; and in America a bare chassis cost a resounding $12,000.

## CADILLAC V-16, 1935

'Brother, can you spare a dime?' might be Top of the Pops in America, but the nation's carriage-trade had embarked on a multi-barrelled spree which expressed itself in terms of six vee-twelves and two vee-sixteens on sale by 1932. The Cadillac in 1935 form was a magnificent brute disposing of 185 b.h.p. from $7\frac{1}{2}$ litres: the valves were overhead with hydraulic lifters, and the result conferred superb smoothness and flexibility. The customer paid in terms of bulk (wheelbase was 12 ft. 10 in.), weight (a good three tons), and thirst (4-5 m.p.g.). If the superb elegance of 1930-1 had succumbed to turret tops and pontoon fenders, Cadillac's coil i.f.s. (another sign of the times) was far superior to the nausea-provoking 'knee action' of General Motors' lesser wares.

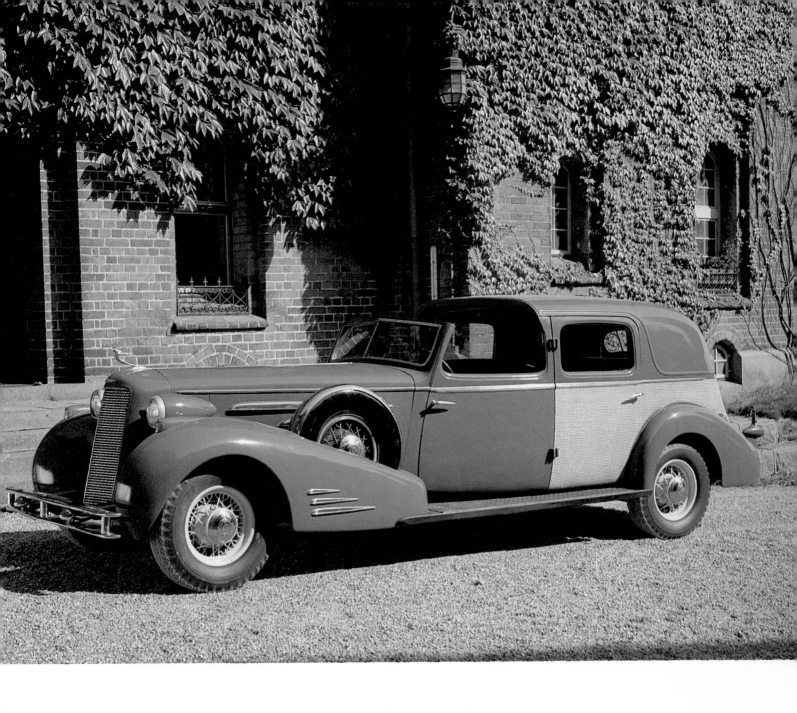

## HORCH '853', 1935

If Isotta Fraschini always played second fiddle to Hispano-Suiza in the Latin world, Germany's Horch was predestined for the role of grooms-man to the big supercharged Mercedes-Benz—a trifle unfair, since the cars from Zwickau were just as well made, if aimed at the tourist rather than the sportsman. Straight-eights were the *specialité de la maison*, and the Fiedler-Schleicher designs of the 1930s had ten-bearing o.h.c. units. In later guise they also had i.f.s., jointed-axle rear suspension, and over-drives for their four-speed synchromesh gearboxes, this last a refine-ment found as early as 1931. The permutations were legion, but the popular sports cabriolet was a heavy car on an 11 ft. 4 in. wheelbase. With only 120 b.h.p. available from 4·9 litres, 85 m.p.h. was hard work. But then it cost a lot fewer Reichsmarks than a 540K!

## BUGATTI TYPE 57C, 1939

By 1934 Ettore Bugatti recognised the demand for refinement in the *grand'routier* class, and he provided it with his Type 57. The 3·3-litre straight-eight engine retained a fixed head and twin upstairs camshafts, but it ran in five plain bearings while a constant-mesh gearbox was used. Bugatti was never one for independent suspension, and hydraulic brakes were not provided until 1938, but the result was good for 95 m.p.h. with saloon coachwork, not to mention a useful 75 on third. The 57C was the same thing *avec compresseur*, and would really go—what price a standing-start hour at 112 m.p.h. in 1939?

## PLEASE SHARE  YOUR THOUGHTS
## ON THIS   BOOK

| comments: | comments: |
|---|---|
| comments: | comments: |
| comments: | comments: |
| comments: | comments: |
| comments: | comments: |
| comments: | comments: |